Love Spells

By

Eden Wilson

Table of contents

Chapter 1

Introduction

The very thing that keeps the globe turning and makes the experience far more delightful is love and for some, love is just that enchanted emotion that transports you to another world where only you two are present. Unfortunately, not everyone has been fortunate enough to find true love, which is the main reason why love charms are a thing.

The exact definition of a love spell is a magical formula that has been specifically created to discover, draw, bond, attract, or even induce love. These spells are not the same as sex magic, sometimes known as "magick." Love spells specifically are meant to attract or create love, although sex magic, on the other hand, sometimes uses sexual feelings and love to achieve outcomes that are either directly or indirectly related to love. For instance, Tantric magick relates to the enlightened state and strives to achieve the union with a god. Love spells, on the other hand, focus more on manipulating a person's feelings for another person.

There aren't any specific kind of love spells. Like regular spells, love spells can range in complexity from straightforward incantations to intricate magical rites. Love spells may be anything from a prayer to a sincere wish. Talismans, amulets, sigils, voodoo dolls, mojos, fetishes, wangas, powders, potions, and philters can all be used in love spells. Love spells may actually take on pretty much any shape you can imagine.

Purpose of Love Spells

Love spells can be used for a variety of things, including:

- Finding and attracting love
- Binding lovers, enhancing and stimulating love
- Maximizing sex appeal

- Beautifying the caster to attract love
- Divining the location or existence of love are all skills that may be used in love spells.

Love spells are the finest tools you can use to accomplish your goals, whether you want to meet your perfect love or ensure that your current relationship will endure a lifetime.

Chapter 2

History of Love Spells

Due to the fact that love spells have been used for many centuries around the world, it is difficult to pinpoint their origin in any one location or culture. This is the main reason why it has been so challenging to trace the origins of love spells. However, if you examine more closely, you'll see that practically all societies have their own distinctive remnants of casting spells in the past.

Love spells now come in two varieties.The first one was based on curses that aim to subdue the Target's will in order to satisfy the Caster's or the person who requested the Caster's help's wish. The second kind, on the other hand, is much more similar to those that are widely practiced today and employ Rituals and Spells to entice someone to fall in love with you.

Greeks prayed to the goddess Aphrodite and made sacrifices to her in an effort to win her approval for their romantic relationships. In order to find the love they want, some people have reached out to those in the magical realms, much like in the other civilizations.
Egyptian magicians and priests, who channeled the gods' will and gave the

populace the assistance they required in terms of love, were comparable to the Greeks' Aphrodite.

Like in most civilizations, offerings and prayers were made to the gods in order for them to grant the demands of the individual making the request for help. While this was happening, the Druids practiced magic using rituals that called for the use of certain plants and other earthen elements.

They held that these organic components were sacred and that they each have a unique power. The majority of these items have been used covertly to unite lovers, while some have been saved for use in the unique wedding rituals. Without a question, love spells have a long history that crosses cultural and geographic boundaries, and each culture and location has its own set of myths and beliefs about them.

There is no disputing the enormous power that love has over people, and love spells are among the most popular spells requested and used to help individuals find the love they have been hoping for. Whatever their pasts may have been, nothing can alter the truth that love is the driving force behind many tales, poems, songs, memoirs, and confessions.

Love is, after all, the very emotion that preserves mankind's humanity.

Chapter 3

Understanding Hellenistic Spells

According to Christopher Faraone, a professor of classics at the University of Chicago who specializes in literature and practices related to magic, men perform Eros magic, whereas women practice Philia magic.

The gender roles of men and women in Ancient Greece can be closely related to these two types of spells. Since women are dependent on their husbands, they have employed the Philia spells. Since women had no authority back then and men had greater flexibility to leave their spouses behind whenever they wanted, ladies employed every trick in the book to make sure their husbands would stick around.Many ladies have utilized Philia charms to preserve their beauty and to retain the necessary tranquility of mind.

Philia magic was employed by women to keep their male partners at bay and faithful. The findings in Philia's love potions, rituals, and spells have disproved the core assumptions about Greek sexual views. These spells were used as a form of treatment or medication rather than for the purpose of obtaining sexual pleasure. The Philia spells are frequently employed by women in an effort to maintain their freshness and beauty in the hopes that doing so will inspire their lover to stay faithful. Many Greek women in antiquity turned to love spells as a kind of healing. If the spells were successful

The women feel considerably more at ease in their current circumstances, giving them a sense of control over the events going on around them. However, the Eros spells have often been utilized by the males and even prostitutes, performing utterly dissimilar roles in the early Greece. The Eros spells have been employed to arouse passion and lust, which will lead them to satisfy the sexual requirements of that person who cast the spell. The ladies had no independence. They simply hoped that things would improve, which explains why they have a history of making spells.

Men, on the other hand, were completely free to do anything they wanted. On the other hand, prostitutes really led lifestyles that were very similar to those of men and women.

These prostitutes had financial freedom and the freedom to live anywhere they wanted, as they were not required to service a particular man or a single household. The only women known to have used the Eros magic to satiate their sexual urges were prostitutes.

Chapter 4

Love Spells In The Renaissance

During this time, magic was no longer treated lightly due to its high cost and the potential for terrible damage to the caster. Simply said, spells were not performed during the Renaissance on just about anyone, but rather only on partnerships that already had a greater significance.

The typical targets of these love charms were gentlemen and ladies of favor and position. A marriage is frequently prevented by constraints based on their social or economic classes, but with the use of love spells, these obstacles may be readily removed, elevating their social position.

The spells were designed to remain hidden, although this has only sometimes been accomplished. But because they themselves believe in magic, the victim will change their behavior once they become aware that they are being cast a spell, which will increase the power of the spell. In a manner, it has evolved into a means of expressing a person's desire, which is significant in the notion of love spells since it provides hesitant people the confidence to approach others who appear impenetrable.

As Christianity and Catholicism predominated the Renaissance in Europe, Christian aspects have also crept into these magical ceremonics. Written magic scrolls and clay dolls are frequently found concealed at church altars or near lighted holy candles during rituals.

In order to accomplish the intended outcomes, the host from the Catholic Mass will occasionally be stolen and utilized throughout the rites. In their most basic form, love charms used throughout the Renaissance are a rich synthesis of paganism and Christianity.

Chapter 5

Casting a love spell

Our actual destiny is love. We don't discover life's purpose on our own; rather, we do so in community.

Today, almost everyone (from men to divorced women) wants to try casting a love spell on the boy of their dreams. It's not just young girls who are interested in doing this.

While many psychics and spellcasters try to convince people that you can't create a love spell by yourself, this isn't totally accurate. If you intend to cast a love spell in order to alter the direction of your love life, there are only a few fundamental guidelines that you need to remember.

- Have faith in what you're planning to do.
- Please offer a prayer to Saint Nicholas, the Miracle Worker, before you carry out the procedure.
- Never attempt to perform a love spell only out of curiosity.
- Only when you really need to do something should you do it.
- You should concentrate on the intended outcome and outcomes when casting a love spell.

- When casting a love spell, take off your shoes, cross yourself, and stay out of the cosmetics.
- Before casting the love spell, make sure no one will annoy you.
- Cast it just how it needs to be cast.
- Be especially careful and precise while combining the ingredients, casting the spell, etc.
- When you are on your period, never perform a love spell.
- Make sure that all of the room's windows and doors are shut when you summon the dead.
- Sunset is the ideal moment to cast a love spell.

- Never divulge the casting of a love spell to anybody.
- Make up a defense against the spell's breaking, such as "tonguc in teeth," "lock in the sea," or "key in the dirt."

Visualizing the visuals associated with the ritual words is one of the key techniques for performing a successful love spell. You must comprehend every word in the spell since they all have significance for you. Think out the words you'll use.
When casting a love spell, it's crucial that you remain as calm as possible. Never restrain your emotions. Even better

results will result from more emotion. Never hold back your enthusiasm or affection since doing so will assist the magic work more faster to grant your request.

Love spells are also said to work best when cast during the new moon and waxing phases of the moon.

It is not advised to perform a spell during the waning of the moon since nature's energy will oppose your request and prevent it from coming true.

Imagine tiny strings of energy coming from your belly button into the belly button of the target of your love spell, where they will then embed themselves in the soul of your sweetheart. This will make the spell more potent.

This can make it much simpler to connect, ensuring that the ritual's effects take effect more quickly.

Once the love spell is complete, ask the Universe to protect your partner from harm.

Chapter 6

Tools Used In Love Spells

Additionally, different love spells require different casting ingredients. Some of the items that are frequently used for love spell casting are listed below. Keep in mind that the supplies you'll need for a ritual will change depending on the type of spell you're casting. You don't need to get ready with all of these items because the list may alter based on the type of love spell you require.

Tools / materials

- Red/pink satin cloth
- Rose petals/rose

- White marbles/stone
- Rose water
- Rosemary leaves
- Olive oil
- Red wine
- Any valued possession that you have
- Cords of different colors
- Candles of different sizes, shapes, and colors
- Photos of casters/partner
- Any incense
- Hair of the caster
- Mirror
- Rock salt
- Needles or any sharp object glass container

In addition to these ingredients, the correct mindset, atmosphere, and surroundings must also exist for the spell to be effective.

Another important element that will impact whether the love spell is successful or unsuccessful is the moon's phase.

Love spells work best at night, ideally between the hours of midnight and one in the morning.

You must also have a dark area or room available while casting love spells.

Chapter 7

Love Spells In Folk Tales

The most common theme in virtually all of the stories you have probably heard throughout your whole life has been love. Love spells are likely to exist whenever there is love. It's likely that even the oldest folk stories ever told include a little amount of the enchantment of love spells.

For instance, the Evil Queen, Snow White's stepmother, may use the magic mirror to become a sorceress, enabling her to not only see everything but also change into a haga to pass for a beggar.

Although she was able to poison Snow White with the apple, the curse was broken by the kiss of pure love, allowing Snow White a chance to recover and find happiness with her Prince Charming. Another factor is the curse that the wicked Fairy Witch pronounced, sending Sleeping Beauty into a deep sleep. The child has been under a death spell since the moment of her birth. But by blocking the magic with her wand, the Good Fairy was able to reduce its impact.

In these folktales, Prince Charming occasionally portrays the hero, but there are other instances in which he portrays the sufferer. There are several stories of witches transforming a gorgeous prince transformed into a frog or other forms of beast, destined to sift through the kingdom to locate a young woman who may end the curse with true love's kiss.

Folklore from many regions of the world is unique in many ways variations of love charms and how they were employed to alter destiny comprising two or more individuals. But in the end, it is unnecessary claiming that pure love, rather than the love spell, is what has liberated the spirits of those individuals who have.

Chapter 8

Love Spells Example

Do charms for love really work? Do any love charms actually work? In short, the answer is a resounding yes, however not all love spells you find will always work flawlessly. The fact is that finding anything that will work requires patience, practice, and a lot of time.

These spells for love are meant to be used when you're looking for a new partner in life. There are various love spell examples that you may attempt that will most effectively serve your needs if you're looking for a spell to help you get your ex back or you need a spell to make your sweetheart come back.

Candle spell for the ideal partner

Casting a love spell with candles is the most romantic thing ever.

The candles won't be lit during the first phase of the spell, but you will notice their flickering flame when the moment is perfect.

Avoid concentrating on a particular individual or mentioning any names when casting this spell. You'll need the following materials:

- One white candle
- One candle of your favorite color
- Candle holders for every candle

- Pink chalk
- Red or pink cloth

If your home doesn't have an altar area, you'll need to find and set up a free area because the spell won't work for several days without it. Hold the white flame while considering the traits you want in a spouse. While focusing on the candle that stands in for your future partner, say them aloud.

Then, using the colored candle to symbolize yourself, consider the attributes you would like to add to this brand-new partnership. The pink fabric should be spread out, and the two candles should be placed with a 2-foot

spacing between them on either side of the cloth. On the pink cloth's middle, between the candles, Create a large heart with the pink chalk. Each night, concentrate on your ideal relationship while focusing on the two candles. Closer together the two candles a little.
Until the two candles are completely around the heart's core, repeat this procedure every night. Although this must last at least one week, the amount of days it takes depends depend on the spacing you select.
Before lighting the two candles, draw another heart around the first one that asks Aphrodite or any other chosen love goddess to fulfill your wish when the two

candles are already side by side inside the heart.

Every night, light them and let them burn until the last candle is gone. Because this love spell could take some time to work, be patient.

Chapter 9

Variations Per Region

Generally speaking, love spells might differ based on local customs of both cultures. Voodoo love spells are completely unrelated to Wiccan love spells. Even if the genuineness of the love charms is still up for debate If you intend to cast a magic, you should exercise caution to fix your love problems aside from the reality that trying to dominate others is unethical, using magical spells or other supernatural means against a person's free will can backfire negatively and have an impact on the person who made the casting spell.

There are several ways to bind the spell in order for the created energy that was put to use for that specific purpose. However, you must be aware that if you want to try to manage a particular individual over an extended length of time, a lot of effort will be required. There are times when the negative energy built up by the magic has a detrimental impact on the person who performed the spell.

The magical and paranormal world has opened up to offer both defensive and offensive magic love spells, reversal spells, and a whole lot more. These include black magic spells, white magic spells, witchcraft, pagan magic, candle or herbal magic, occult magic that invokes spirits, use of amulets, talismans, charms, stones, potions, and many others.

The energy is channeled via the objects or symbols used in magical love spells in order to bring about the desired transformation or achieve a certain goal. All objects in our world have their own dynamic energy, according to spell specialists.
These can assist in creating greater energy that will then be directed into influencing an event's natural path

through the employment of various psychological methods.
Metals, plants, planetary combinations, artifacts, musical notes, and other symbols are only aids in evoking specific emotions and serving as symbols for particular concepts.

Casting love spells requires mental fortitude as well as the development of psychological tools like visualization, projection, and focus.
The spells can support a person in recognizing, emphasizing, dealing with, and even discarding their hidden anxieties and complexes. As a result, one

will be able to speak more effectively with one's inner self.

www.ingramcontent.com/pod-product-compliance
Lightning Source LLC
LaVergne TN
LVHW020533160826
845677LV00015B/4030
9798847052542